Wl
Want To Be

by Bernadette Meyers

illustrated by Karen Dugan

HOUGHTON MIFFLIN HARCOURT
School Publishers

Printed in China

ISBN-13: 978-0-547-02719-7
ISBN-10: 0-547-02719-2

2 3 4 5 6 7 8 0940 18 17 16 15 14 13 12 11 10

Today I decided what I want to be when I grow up. In the morning I told my sister Elena.

"I know what I want to be!" I said.

"You do?" asked Elena.

I said, "Yes, I want to be a dancer just like you!"

"Then you should come to practice with me, Sophia," said Elena. "You can see the work I do every day."

So I went to practice with
Elena. She stretched and jumped.
She stood on her toes and twirled.

I tried to do everything she did,
but it was too hard. I almost
fell down.

I felt tired and sweaty when
we were done. Dancing is very
hard work!

"Maybe I won't be a dancer after all," I said. "Your work is very tiring."

"Let's talk about it at lunch," said Elena.

We went to a restaurant and saw our neighbor Alicia. She is a chef at the restaurant. When she brought us our food, I had an idea.

"Alicia," I said, "I know what I want to be when I grow up. I want to be a chef."

"Really?" she laughed. "Then you should come to the kitchen soon and watch what I do."

"That's a great idea!" I said.

After lunch, I went to the kitchen with Alicia. Everyone was rushing and yelling.

Alicia had fun cooking, but I didn't have much fun watching her. The kitchen was too noisy and hot for me.

Then I saw a reporter eating at a table. He was writing about the restaurant.

I had an idea. I could be a reporter! Reporters look for news, and then they write a story. They just need <mark>paper</mark> and a pencil!

Later, I looked for news in
my neighborhood. I saw workers
building a new playground.

This is news! I thought.

I had my paper and pencil with
me, so I drew a lot of pictures. I
didn't have time to write any words.

At dinner, I told my family about the reporter at the restaurant. I showed them my drawings of the playground.

"You have done a lot of work on these drawings! Will you be a reporter one day?" Elena asked.

"No," I said. "I changed my mind. I want to be an artist!"

Responding

✔ **TARGET SKILL** **Conclusions**

Sophia decides to become an artist. What three details make her come to this conclusion? Make a chart.

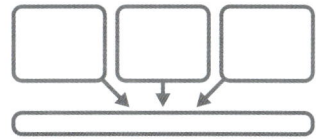

✏ Write About It

Text to Text Think about the work people do in a different story. Write two sentences that tell how the jobs in that story are different from the jobs in this story.

WORDS TO KNOW

done	paper	were
great	soon	work
laughs	talks	

LEARN MORE WORDS

artist	dancer	reporter

TARGET SKILL **Conclusions**

Use details to figure out more about the text.

TARGET STRATEGY **Monitor/Clarify**

Find ways to figure out what doesn't make sense.

GENRE **Realistic fiction** is a story that could happen in real life.